The purpose of this book is to assist readers become well informed healthcare consumers. It is provided as overall health care advice.

It is always suggested that you seek medical advice from your personal physician before starting any fresh workout program.

This book is not designed to be a replacement for a certified physician's medical recommendation. In all issues pertaining to his / her health, the reader should check with their doctor. **Note:** This is a book and not a product. Be guided!

DISCLAIMER

By reading this disclaimer, you are accepting the terms of this disclaimer in full. If you disagree with this disclaimer, please do not order or read this book. The content in this book is provided for information and educational purposes only. Therefore this book is not intended to be used as a substitute for medical application whatsoever.

All products names, diet plans used in this book are for identification purposes only and are property of their respective owners. The use of these names does not imply endorsement. All other trademarks cited herein are the property of their respective owners.

None of the information in this book should be adopted as an independent medical or other professional advice. The information in this book has been compiled from different sources that are deemed reliable. Proper analysis and summary to the best of author's knowledge and belief has been done to achieve this book. However, the author cannot guarantee the accuracy and thus should not be held liable for any errors.

You acknowledge and agree that by continuing to read this book, you will (where applicable, appropriate, or necessary) consult a qualified medical professional on this information. The information in this book is not intended to be any sort of medical advice and should not be used in lieu of any medical advice by a licensed and qualified medical professional.

Lastly, do not interpret this book or its content for a medication. This is only a book guide. God bless you as you comply.

Table of Contents

INTRODUCTION

The Rice Diet is majorly about healthy carbohydrates. High-fiber vegetables, fruits, and grains; only fruit and grains are recommended to be eaten on "detox" days. No qualms, this Diet is also low in salt and low in fat.

For the first phase of this Rice Diet it is expected you lose weight because you are limited to about 800 calories per day, which is very low, take in 1,600 calories per day to maintain good nutrition. The Rice Diet also detoxifies the body, ridding it of excess water weight and toxins from processed foods and the environment.

After the detoxification stage, you stay on about 1,000 calories per day until you achieve your desired weight. In the final phase, which is maintenance, calories go up a little more, but the diet continues to be low on calories, fat, and salt and high on fruit, vegetables, and grains.

Rice

One of the oldest cereal grains, rice (Oryza sativa) is believed to have been grown for at least 5000 years. It is a staple food for more than half of the world's population, particularly those living in southern and eastern Asia.

White rice is the most commonly consumed type, but brown (whole grain) rice is becoming increasingly popular in some Western countries due to its health benefits.

Various products are made from rice. These include rice flour, rice syrup, rice bran oil, and rice milk. It is usually white in color, but brown rice can come in a variety of shades; brown, reddish, purplish, or black

It is the major food crop in the world. Nearly 40% of the world population consumes rice as the major staple food. Most of the people, who depend on rice as primary food, live in the less developed countries.

Archeological evidence on rice in India dates back to 1500-1000 B.C. Since the dawn of civilization, rice has served humans as a life-giving cereal in the humid regions of Asia and, to a lesser extent, in West Africa. Introduction of rice into Europe and the America has led to its increased use in human diets. There are 42 rice producing countries throughout the world but China and India are major rice production centers. Rice is grown in wide range of agro-climatic conditions ranging from mountainous (Jammu) lands to low land delta areas (Sundarban), spanning an area from 53° latitude north to 35° south of the world but about 90% of the crop is grown and consumed in Asia.

Rice provides fully 60% of the food intake in Southeast Asia and about 35% in East Asia and South Asia. The highest level of per capita rice consumption (130-180 kg per year, 55-80% of total caloric source) takes place in Bangladesh, Cambodia, Indonesia, Laos, Myanmar (Burma), Thailand, and Vietnam (Kenneth and Kriemhild, 2000). In many cultures of the world rice are the central part of people's life and culture. Rice is an excellent food and is an excellent source of carbohydrates and energy. During last 50years, world rice area has increased by 1.37 times from 115.50 to 159 m ha but production has increased three times from 216 to 685 mt and productivity has increased 2.3 times from 1.87 t/ha to 4.30 t/ha . China is the world's leading rice producer with nearly 125 million tones production. India possess largest rice area (45 m ha) producing nearly a quarter of Asia's production occupying second position after China

In India, Rice production and productivity showed a steady increase from the first five year plan to the tenth five year plan. Rice production has been increased during last six decades by nearly 481% or 4.8 times from 20.58mt in 1950-51 to nearly 99.15mt during 2008-09, whereas the average rice productivity has been increased 3.3 folds from 668 kg/ha in 1950-51 to 2186 kg/ha in 2008-09.

As a human food, rice continues to gain popularity in many parts of the world where other coarse cereals, such as maize, sorghum and millet, or tubers and roots like potatoes, yams, and cassava have traditionally dominated. For example, of all the world's regions, Africa has had the sharpest rise in rice consumption during the last few decades. Rice is unquestionably a superior source of energy among the cereals. The protein quality of rice (66%) ranks only below that of oats (68%) and surpasses that of whole wheat (53%) and of corn (49%). Milling of brown rice into white rice results in a nearly 50% loss of the vitamin-B-complex and iron and washing milled rice prior to cooking further reduces the water-soluble vitamin content. However, the amino acids, especially lysine, are less affected by the milling process.

Rice, which is low in sodium and fat and is free of cholesterol, serves as an aid in preventing hypertension. It is also free from allergens and now widely used in baby foods. Because rice flour is nearly pure starch and free from allergens, it is the main component of face powders and infant formulas. Its low fibre content has led to an increased use of rice powder in polishing camera lenses and expensive jeweler. Rice starch can also serve as a substitute for glucose in oral rehydration solution for infants suffering from diarrhoea. The coarse and silica-rich rice hull is finding new use in construction materials. Rice straw is used less in rope and paper making industries than before, but except for modern varieties, it still serves as an important cattle feed throughout Asia. In industrial usage, rice is also gaining importance in the making of infant foods, snack foods, breakfast cereals, beer, fermented products, and rice bran oil, and rice wine remains a major alcoholic beverage in East Asia.

How White Rice is Good for the Body

1. White Rice Can Actually Help Stabilize Blood Sugar Levels

That may be odd to hear as white rice is mostly starch and fairly high on the glycemic index. The glycemic index is commonly used to rank foods based on how they affect blood sugar. High glycemic foods such as sodas, fruit juices, sweetened breakfast cereals, candy, white bread and yes, white rice, can spike blood sugar levels more easily than other foods. Over time, high blood sugar can lead to weight gain and type II diabetes.

2. White Rice is Easy to Digest

Most people don't know that whole grains can be hard for the body to digest (including most doctors) if they're not properly prepared. The outer layer of all grains contains something called phytic acid which is an anti-nutrient and can cause digestive distress if it's not neutralized.

Nature does this when a grain (which is essentially a seed) hits the earth and sprouts into a new plant.

Moisture, warmth and other soil conditions will naturally release the bran. Traditionally, cultures all around the world learned to mimic Nature by soaking, sprouting and fermenting grains. These proper preparations neutralize phytic acid (as well as other anti-nutrients in the bran) and make grains much more digestible.

But few people do this anymore because of the time involved and few food companies do this for the same reason (time is money when you're a business). But this is not a problem with white rice as the bran has already been removed. People with chronic digestive issues will have a much easier time digesting white rice.

3. White Rice Does Not Contain Gluten

Or any of the other possibly problematic compounds that are a part of the three main sources of gluten wheat, barley and rye. No one knows exactly why gluten is causing so many health problems today. It could be that gluten itself is a complex and difficult protein for the body to digest. It could be that it's in so much junk food and that we eat so much of it. It could be the new modern hybrids of wheat which are thought to be higher in gluten than more historical strains. It could be the chemicals that are sprayed on wheat. Or it could be a combination of all those things.

Whatever the reasons, it's a food that more and more people are becoming sensitive to. However, white rice is a very hypoallergenic food and presents none of those issues and is perfectly acceptable if you're on a gluten-free diet.

4. White Rice Can Help with Chronic Digestive Issues

Beyond its digestibility, many eastern healing systems look at white rice as having certain qualities or energetic characteristics that can be beneficial. For example, both Ayurveda, the ancient healing system of India, and Traditional Chinese Medicine, consider it a Yin or cooling food that can help clear excessive heat and thus settle digestive upset in its many forms.

Those from Asian countries know this well. Congee, a simple meal of white rice and bone broth, has countless variations throughout Asia and has been used for thousands of years for healing gut issues.

Brown Rice

The unpolished and unrefined form of white rice is known as brown rice. This variety is obtained by removing just the outer hull of the kernel of rice and retains the layer of nutrient filled bran. The brown and unrefined variety is definitely superior to the staple white and refined one in a many ways. Most importantly, is the abundance of essential nutrients that come with brown rice, which is more often than not lost in the multiple milling and polishing in white rice's case.

It as an excellent source of manganese, and a good source of selenium, phosphorus, copper, magnesium, and niacin (vitamin B3). Not contain gluten, which is typical of almost all other cereals and cause allergies.

Types of Brown Rice:
Brown rice is also available in different varieties. But all of it is said to be very good for your health. Here are some of the different varieties or types of brown rice that you need to try.

1. Medium Grain Brown Rice:

This rice is larger and appears to be plump-like than the usual small variety. Once this type of rice is cooked it tends to becomes tender and moist. This tastes well with soups and salads. This type of brown rice usually takes 15 to 20 minutes to cook.

2. Short Grain Type of Brown Rice:

This type of brown rice has a sticky texture once it is cooked. However, this rice takes 25 minutes to cook even after being soaked overnight. This works well with some sambar and dal. Short grain type of brown rice aids helps you reduce your weight.

3. Light Brown Coloured Brown Rice:

This type of brown rice is called light brown because half of its bran is removed when it has been milled. Thus, this rice appears in the colour of light brown and gives a nutty taste once it is cooked. This rice has fewer fibre when compared to short grain and medium grain. It take just 20 minutes to cook this rice.

4. Long Brown Rice:

This type of brown rice is something similar to that of basmati rice and appears to be golden brown in colour. Its taste is similar to that of light brown rice and is common used in most dishes around the world.

This rice takes a minimum of 45 minutes to cook. Moreover, this rice is said to be very healthy for you.

Benefits of Brown Rice for Skin, Hair & Health

There are numerous benefits of including brown rice in your diet, not just for your health, but also for skin and hair!

Skin

Did you know that your blood sugar levels and the health of your skin are related? Brown rice offers you the right amount of vitamin B, as opposed to white rice that contains carbohydrates. It also includes antioxidants and minerals that keep the skin soft and smooth.

- Flawless Skin
- Stalls Premature Aging
- Maintains Skin's Elasticity
- Treats Acne
- Cures Eczema
- Soothes Rashes And Sunburns

Hair

- Heals Damaged Hair
- Works As A Natural Hair Conditioner
- Treats Dandruff

Health

1. Controls Cholesterol Level
2. Protects From Free Radical Damage
3. Prevents Heart Diseases
4. Beneficial For Diabetics
5. Helps To Control Weight
6. Prevents Cancer
7. Prevents Neuro-Degenerative Complications
8. Treats Insomnia
9. Prevents Gallstones
10. Bone Health
11. Beneficial For Nervous System
12. Cures Asthma
13. Keeps The Immune System Strong
14. Beneficial For Lactating Women
15. Contains Anti-Depressant Qualities
16. Aids Proper Bowel Function

17. Controls Candida Yeast Infections
18. Is Perfect As A Baby Food

Black Rice/ Forbidden Rice

Black rice, also called purple rice, forbidden rice, and Chinese black rice is a type of whole-grain rice that is quite dark in color. It can be completely black or more of a dark purple or burgundy with some multicolored kernels. When black rice is cooked, it turns dark purple.

Forbidden rice is non-glutinous heirloom rice. It has a dark purplish-black color with a nutty, slightly sweet flavor. Is black rice really rice? As odd as it may look if you've never seen it before, it is certainly a type of rice.

Forbidden rice includes a range of rice types that all belong to the species Oryza sativa, some of which are glutinous rice. Thai black rice, for example also called black sticky rice or black glutinous rice has a sticky texture and is often used in desserts in Thai cuisine.

Glutinous or sticky rices have higher amounts of amylopectin, which makes them very sticky when cooked. Black Japonica rice is a mix of Asian black short-grain rice and medium-grain mahogany rice grown together in the same field.

It is often considered a superfood because of its high nutritional content, in addition to the fact that it's naturally high in anthocyanins, which are the antioxidant pigments that give the rice its unique coloring. In Traditional Chinese Medicine, it's even considered a blood tonic.

Can you eat black rice on keto? Unfortunately, rices of all kinds are typically a "no" on the ketogenic diet. The good news? Black forbidden rice is an option for those following a gluten-free diet.

Health Benefits of Black Rice

A driving force of antioxidants, protein, iron, vitamins and minerals; this rice has enormous health benefits, which makes it a perfect healthy option to go for! Here's how the consumption of this magical superfood helps in preventing from various diseases and promotes good health.

Works as a natural detoxifier: Hectic lifestyle, junk eating habits and use of various substances often lead to several life threatening diseases. However, natural detoxification often helps in preventing several diseases. Black rice is a rich source of phytonutrients, which works as a natural detoxifier and pulls out disease causing free radicals from the body. You can also add beetroot and noni to your diet, as they are loaded with detoxifying properties.

Good for Liver: One of the pivotal organs of our body is the liver, which performs several functions that help in proper functioning of the digestive system. Black rice helps in detoxifying the body and extracting all the toxin particles with antioxidant activities

Helps in weight loss: Apart from being rich in antioxidants, black rice is a great source of fiber. One cup of black rice has approx 6 grams of fiber, which helps the body to stay satiated and makes you feel full even if you consume small quantities of it. Moreover, the high-fiber content of black rice helps in easing out the bowel movements, relieves bloating, diarrhea and prevents constipation. The soluble fiber of black rice binds with the toxins and effectively pulls out the waste from the body. This further leads to weight loss.

Helps keep diabetes at bay: Patients with high sugar levels are often advised to cut down on sugar as well as carbohydrates. It is often advised to go for whole grains rather than going for refined carbs. Well, black rice is high on fiber and low in carbs, which makes it an apt choice for diabetes patients. In fact, the bran, which is the outer coating of rice has the majority of fiber content. The fiber of black rice helps the body to absorb the glucose over a long period of time, which further helps in maintaining a balance of sugar level.

Difference between Black Rice and Brown Rice

Black Rice

Black rice has a unique flavor and a glossy ebony color. The outer layer of black rice contains bran, which is rich in antioxidants. These antioxidants are like the ones contained in acai berries, grapes and blueberries. They're called anthocyanins; and they've been linked to cancer prevention, improved memory and a lowered risk of heart disease. Black rice is now gaining ground as a new "superfood." Not only is it gaining fans in the kitchen, but researchers are now recommending it for its health benefits.

Brown Rice

Basically, brown rice is white rice before it's been processed. The outside bran is intact, which means that it contains the bran fiber, minerals, vitamins and many other nutrients. It's also high in Omega-3 and Omega-6 fatty acids. Brown rice has been linked to weight loss and a lowered risk of diabetes. It's high in fiber, so it promotes more effective metabolic function and helps to keep your blood sugar stabilized.

- Black rice has twice the amount of protein of brown rice.
- It is twice the amount of fiber of brown rice.
- With twice the amount of iron of brown rice.
- Black rice also has other powerful antioxidants, such as zeaxanthin and lutein that, which are great for vision.

How to cook Black Rice

What makes black rice a much preferred healthy grain is the umpteen health benefits it offers! However, over cooking it can result in loss of essential vitamins, minerals and antioxidants. There are three basic techniques that can be used for cooking almost all hard grains the absorption method, the pasta method, and the pilaf method. Here is how you can use these methods for cooking black rice:

The Absorption Method

The absorption method is the most basic and popular method of cooking grains.

This technique requires the grain to be cooked in a specific quantity of liquid that should be fully absorbed by the grain by the end of cooking. When using the absorption method, you can also use broth instead of water to give the dish more flavor.

The Ingredients:

- 2 1/4 cup water or broth
- 1 cup of black rice, rinsed
- 1/8 tsp of salt (or to taste)

Instruction

To cook black rice using the absorption method, add water, and rinsed black rice to a saucepan. Over medium-high heat, bring the water to a boil. Add the salt, reduce heat, cover, and cook for about 30-35 minutes.

Resist the urge to open the lid too often to check on the rice because this will let a lot of steam out. Continue cooking until the rice is tender and chewy, and all water is absorbed. Take off the heat and let it stand covered for about 5 to 10 minutes, then fluff with a fork and serve.

Troubleshooting:

If all the water has evaporated, but the rice is not fully cooked yet, add 2 to 3 tablespoons of water and cook for 5 more minutes.

Keep in Mind:

The time and water to rice ratio required to cook the perfect black rice using the absorption method very much depend on the amount of water that evaporates during cooking. And this, in turn, depends on your cooking environment, such as the saucepan and lid you are using, the humidity in your area, the altitude you live in, etc. So, you might need to experiment to determine the ratio and timing that works best for you.

The Pasta Method

The pasta method of cooking hard grains isn't very popular, but it is super easy and works very well with black rice.

This technique requires the grain to be cooked just like pasta in a large amount of water in a pot without a lid. When the grain is cooked, the water is discarded.

It's is an excellent method of cooking black rice because you don't have to figure out and remember the exact ratio of water to rice.

It results in the black rice with a very nice non-sticky consistency. It's also more flexible as you can taste the rice during cooking to check for doneness. In addition, you don't have to worry about burning the rice or getting a hard crust at the bottom of the pan.

The disadvantages of this method are that you can only use water and not broth for cooking as you will be discarding it at the end, and some nutrients will also be lost in the discarded water.

The Ingredients:

- 6 cups of water
- 1 tsp of salt
- 1 cup of black rice, rinsed

Instruction

To cook black rice using the pasta method, add the water, rinsed black rice, and salt to a large pot. Bring to a boil and cook for about 30 to 35 minutes until the rice is tender and chewy. Strain the black rice using a mesh colander.

The Pilaf Method

In the pilaf method, grains are lightly toasted in oil with aromatics such as vegetables, herbs, and spices first and then simmered in water or stock.

To prepare a fragrant pilaf, you can use carrots, onion, shallots, garlic, ginger, fennel, celery, green peas, bay leaves, cumin, thyme, etc. You can also experiment by cooking the black rice pilaf with chicken or vegetable stock instead of water.

The Ingredients:

- 1 Tbsp olive oil
- 1/4 medium onion, thinly sliced
- 1 garlic clove, minced
- 1 cup black rice
- 2 1/4 cup water
- 1/8 tsp salt (or to taste)

Instruction

In a saucepan, heat the oil over medium heat. Add the onion and cook stirring occasionally until the onion is translucent for about 2 minutes, then add the garlic and cook for about 30 seconds.

Add the black rice and cook, stirring until the grains are well coated in oil and become fragrant. Then add the water and salt and bring to a boil.

Reduce heat, cover, and cook until the black rice is tender and chewy for about 30 to 35 minutes. Take the rice off the heat and let it stand covered for about 5 to 10 minutes, then fluff with a fork and serve.

Troubleshooting:

If all the water has evaporated, but the rice is not fully cooked yet, add 2 to 3 tablespoons of water and cook for 5 more minutes.

Keep in Mind:

The time and water to rice ratio required to cook the perfect black rice pilaf very much depend on the amount of water that evaporates during cooking. And this, in turn, depends on your cooking environment, such as the saucepan and lid you are using, the humidity in your area, the altitude you live in, etc. So, you might need to experiment to determine the ratio and timing that works best for you.

Side Effect of Black Rice

Black rice does not have any serious documented side effects. Talk to your doctor before taking black rice extract if you are nursing and pregnant. Because it's rich in fiber, it may cause slight bloating, gas, or gastrointestinal upset; this should subside quickly.

RICE DIET

The rice diet is a high-complex carb, low-fat, and low-sodium diet. A simple diet of rice and fruit could treat a host of medical conditions, including kidney failure. Altering the diet could reduce stress on the kidneys and effectively treat renal failure. The best way to do this was to drastically reduce protein intake, since the kidneys are largely responsible for processing protein.

Cutting out sodium and cholesterol could lower blood pressure and improve heart failure. Rice and fruit protocol was a daily diet consisting almost entirely of carbohydrates with very low amounts of protein and virtually no sodium or cholesterol.

Also, the Rice Diet is the basis for a medically-supervised, live-in program designed for rapid weight-loss over a period of 2 to 4 weeks or more, in the treatment of obesity, diabetes, heart disease, hypertension, and renal disease. The Rice Diet is not like fad diets which come and go, but has developed into a complete, proven and well-respected program for improving health.

As well as meals using the Rice Diet, the program provides classes, groups and workshops for stress management and exercise, nutritional lectures, and personal medical supervision.

If you choose a low-calorie diet for weight loss, it's important to meet daily nutritional needs. Adults should get at least 130 grams of carbs, 46 to 56 grams of protein (a minimum for women and men, respectively), and at least 20 percent of their daily calories from dietary fat. With the exception of day 1, meal and menu plan below contain 900 to 1,200 calories and meet macronutrient (carb, protein and fat) recommendations. Diets containing 800 calories or fewer daily require medical supervision.

Portion Sizes

When following the rice diet, use the following portion sizes:

- 1 fruit portion: 1 cup of fruit or 1 medium piece of fruit

- 1 veggie portion: 1 cup of raw or cooked non-starchy veggies
- 1 starch portion: 1 slice of bread, 1 cup of ready-to-eat cereal, or 1/2 cup of cooked rice, pasta, quinoa, dry beans or oatmeal
- 1 dairy portion: 1 cup of low-fat milk, yogurt, or 1/2 cup of cottage cheese
- 1 fat portion: 1 teaspoon of oils, or 1 tablespoon of nuts

Day 1 (All Phases) Meal Plan and Sample Menu

Regardless of which phase you're in on the Rice Diet, day one remains the same: eating about 800 to 1,000 calories per day, and choosing two starches and two fruits at each meal.

- **Breakfast:** 2 starches and 2 fruits (1 cup of cooked oatmeal, one cup of strawberries and small orange)
- **Lunch:** 2 starches and 2 fruits (1/2 cup of cooked rice, 1/2 cup black beans, 1 cup of blueberries and 1 cup of melon)

- **Dinner:** 2 starches and 2 fruits (1 cup of cooked quinoa, 1 cup of sliced apples and kiwi fruit)

Phases 1 and 2 Meal Plan

During phases 1 and 2 (with the exception of day 1), use the following meal plan containing about 900 to 1,000 calories per day:

- Breakfast: 1 starch, 1 fruit and 1 low-fat dairy serving
- Lunch: 2 starches, 2 fat, 1 vegetable and 1 fruit serving
- Dinner: 1 starch, 1 fat, 2 vegetables and 1 fruit serving

Phase 1 or 2 Sample Menu

Using the meal plan above, try this sample menu:

- Breakfast: 1 slice of toast, 1 cup of raspberries, and 1 cup of low-fat Greek yogurt

- Lunch: 1/2 cup of cooked rice, 1/2 cup of pinto beans, 2 teaspoons of oil, 1 cup of Brussels sprouts, and 1 plum
- Dinner: 1/2 cup cooked quinoa, 1 teaspoon of oil, 1 cup of carrots, 1 cup of celery, and 1 cup of pineapple

Phase 3 Meal Plan

When following the least restrictive phase of the rice diet (phase three), try the following meal plan:

- Breakfast: 1 fruit, 1 starch, 1 dairy, and 1 fat serving
- Snack: 1 dairy serving
- Lunch: 2 veggie, 2 starch, and 1 fat serving
- Snack: 1 fruit serving
- Dinner: 1 vegetable, 1 starch, 3 ounces of fish, poultry or seafood, and 1 fat serving

Phase 3 Sample Menus

The following menus are derived from the original rice diet phase 3, but are well-balanced enough to help meet adults' daily nutritional needs.

Day 1

- Breakfast: 1 small banana, 1 cup of whole-grain cereal, 1 cup of low-fat milk, and 1 tablespoon of walnuts
- Snack: 1 cup of cottage cheese
- Lunch: 2 cups of steamed asparagus, 1/2 cup of cooked rice, 1/2 cup of cooked black beans, and 1 teaspoon of oil (or try a black beans and rice recipe)
- Snack: 1 small apple
- Dinner: 1 cup green of beans, 1/2 cup of cooked quinoa, 3 ounces of salmon, and 1 teaspoon of oil

Day 2

- Breakfast: 1 cup of honeydew melon, 1/2 cup cooked oatmeal, 1 cup of soy milk, and 1 tablespoon of sliced almonds
- Snack: 1 cup of non-fat plain Greek yogurt
- Lunch: 2 cups of celery and carrot sticks, 1/2 cup of cooked rice, 1/2 cup of cooked pinto beans, and 1 teaspoon of oil (or try a red beans and rice recipe)
- Snack: 1 cup of blueberries
- Dinner: 1 cup of steamed broccoli, 3 ounces of grilled chicken, 1/2 cup of brown rice, and 1 teaspoon of oil

Day 3

- Breakfast: 1 cup of raspberries, 1 slice of whole-grain toast, 1 tablespoon of cashew butter, and 1 cup of low-fat milk
- Snack: 1 cup of non-fat plain Greek yogurt

- Lunch: 1 cup of tomatoes, 1 cup of cucumbers, 1/2 cup of cooked rice, 1/2 cup of cooked garbanzo beans, and 1 teaspoon of oil
- Snack: 1 cup of pineapple
- Dinner: 1 cup of peppers sauteed in 1 teaspoon of olive oil, 1/2 cup cooked quinoa, and 3 ounces of grilled shrimp (or, try this quinoa and garlic shrimp recipe)

How the Rice Diet works

The diet works by focusing on limiting salt and foods high in sodium. This will help your body de-bloat and shed excess water weight. In combination with eating low-sodium foods, the diet also limits saturated fats.

Instead, it uses high-fiber foods to fill you up and carbs like fruit, vegetables, grains, and beans, as the main source of nutrition. It also limits almost all dairy from your diet.

The rice diet plan also follows a calorie allowance if you're looking to lose weight. Initially, it recommends starting at a lower calorie level and then building up to around 1,200 to 1,500 calories per day if you're not exercising.

If you follow the diet plan presented in the book, you go through three phrases that teach portion control and how to balance food so you can have the freedom to eat whatever you want in moderation.

Eating grains and fruits for one day of the week and adding foods like vegetables and beans for the rest of the days.

The guidelines for rice diet plan involves eating per day:

- 1,000 calories
- 500 to 1,000 mg of sodium
- 22 g of fat
- 5.5 g of saturated fat
- 0 to 100 mg of cholesterol

And like most in-depth weight management programs, the diet focuses on lifestyle changes, like keeping a food journal and exploring your relationship with food, your body, and self through meditation, self-awareness, and diet.

Effectiveness

In general, following any type of meal plan that reduces calories and focuses on vegetables and lean protein will be effective in helping you lose weight. However, it's also important to make sure you're eating enough calories, too. Depending on your metabolism and exercise and activity levels, eating too few calories can actually have the opposite effect on weight loss

The Short Term and Long-Term Effect of Rice Diet

Rice Diet is good for short-term benefits. Eating a carbohydrate-rich diet with less salt and less of processed foods can be good in the short-term. However, in the long term due to a low amount of calories or protein most people find it difficult to sustain. After the target weight is reached you should slowly shift to a more traditional diet and try to maintain weight by adopting healthy eating habits and lifestyle.

SAMPLE MENU

The Rice Diet menu is divided into starches, fruits, vegetables, and dairy. In this sample menu, a starch serving can be one slice of bread, one-third cup of rice, or one-half cup of pasta. A fruit is one whole fruit or a cup of fruit. One vegetable is one cup uncooked or one-half cup cooked. Dairy is one cup of milk or yogurt or one-half cup of cottage cheese. This sample menu is from the phase of the diet that restricts protein. Later on, fish and lean meats may be added.

• Breakfast: your choice of one serving of starch, non-fat dairy, and fruit
• Lunch: three starches, three vegetables, and one fruit
• Dinner: same as lunch

Savory Rice

This Easy Savoury Rice is easy to prepare, quick, healthy and tasty. It is made from simple ingredients that you will probably have in your fridge/cupboards already. It also comes together from start to finish in under thirty minutes, like my so is great for those days when you have limited time available for preparing dinner.

Feel free to swap out any of the vegetables or to add some extras. Frozen sweetcorn is great instead of or as well as the peas.

This Easy Savoury Rice is great on it's own as a meal or it can be used as a side. Try it with some crispy tofu and a drizzle of sweet chilli sauce, or if you have children they might enjoy it with a good quality meat free sausage on the side.

Ingredients

- 1 tablespoon oil , optional - You can saute in a few tablespoons of water instead if you prefer to be oil-free

- 1 medium onion , chopped finely
- 4 cloves garlic , chopped finely
- 1 small fresh chilli , or dried, (you can omit this if you don't want any heat)
- 1 large carrot , diced
- 1 medium bell pepper , diced
- 150g | 1 cup frozen peas
- 10 grape tomatoes
- 1 cup uncooked rice (any rice will do, white, brown, long grain, short grain, risotto rice)
- 480mls | 2 cups vegetable stock
- Salt and pepper to taste

Instructions

- Add the oil/water to a pan and heat on medium.
- Add the onion and sauté until softened and just starting to colour.
- Add the garlic and chili and sauté for 1 minute more

- Add the carrot, bell pepper and rice and stir until the rice starts to make slight popping sounds.
- Add the stock.
- Add the grape tomatoes and peas.
- Stir well and cover with a lid.
- Let simmer for about 20-25 minutes or until the rice is tender and the liquid has mostly absorbed. Stir every so often so the rice doesn't stick to the bottom of the pan.
- Note that if you are using brown rice or wild rice it might take slightly longer to cook through.
- Season with salt and pepper to taste.
- Serve immediately.

Notes

Nutritional information is calculated on the recipe serving 2 people but it could easily stretch to 3.

Black Rice Pudding

Creamy black rice pudding is the perfect vegan, gluten-free decadent breakfast, snack or dessert. Black rice is cooked with coconut milk, coconut sugar, and spices until creamy. It is topped with coconut flakes, banana, and mango slices to create such a satisfying dish.

Ingredients

- 1 cup black rice
- 2 1/2 cups water
- 14 ounce can coconut milk
- 1/2 cup coconut sugar
- 1/4 teaspoon salt
- 1 teaspoon vanilla
- 1/4 teaspoon cinnamon

Instructions

1. Sort black rice to remove debris. Place the rice in a fine mesh strainer and wash rice under cold running water. Transfer the rice to a pot with water, coconut milk, coconut sugar, and salt.

2. Bring to a boil, reduce to simmer, and cover the pot and cook for 45 minutes. Stir in the cinnamon and vanilla, and allow rice pudding to cook for 10 more minutes or until most of the liquid has evaporated.

3. To serve rice pudding warm, divide rice pudding into 8 bowls and serve garnished with mango slices, coconut flakes, and banana. You can store rice pudding in the refrigerator in a container with a lid, and it will keep for 3 days when chilled.

Notes

- Sweeten your rice pudding to taste, start by using 1/4 cup and increase.
- Substitute maple syrup, stevia, organic cane sugar, or another sweetener of choice.
- Make sure to use black rice and not wild rice, as they are not the same.
- Rice pudding will further thicken as it cools.
- Reduce the cooking time by soaking the rice overnight in cold water.
- The health benefits of black rice are in the bran, so make sure to purchase the whole grain

so you can get the maximum benefit of black rice.

Fried Rice

Fried rice is a delicious, stir-fried dish. The vegetables used in fried rice usually differ based on preference, but carrots and onions are usually the most commonly used.

Fried rice is a versatile dish that can be prepared in a variety of ways with a wide range of ingredients. If you like this recipe, you might also want give Coconut fried rice, Chinese-style Egg fried rice or even Beef fried rice a try!

Ingredients

- 500g long grain white rice
- 500ml of Chicken or Turkey stock
- 100g Cow Liver (use beef as a substitute)
- 2 large Carrots
- 1 handful of Green Peas
- 1 large Green bell pepper (Green pepper)
- 1 Onion bulb

- 2-3 tablespoonfuls of Curry Powder
- 1 teaspoonful of Garlic Powder (optional)
- 1/2 a tablespoonful of black of white pepper (optional)
- 2-3 cooking spoonful of Pure Vegetable Oil
- 2 seasoning cubes
- Salt to taste

Method

Step 1

Place the Chicken in a pot, add 1 teaspoon thyme, 1 teaspoon curry, 1 stock cube and onion slices. Add a little water and cook the chicken for 10 minutes. Then add more water and cook until done. The liquid left after cooking the chicken, is your stock. Pour the stock into a Strainer to remove tiny chicken bones and any other particles in it; then set the stock aside for later use.

Step 2

Fry or grill the chicken.

Step 3

Wash and place the cow liver in a pot, add seasoning cube and salt to taste; Cook the liver for 10minutes, then when cooled, cut into cubes and set aside. Liver can also be fried, before cutting into cubes. (Tip: If you can't stand liver, you can use fried beef, chicken or shrimps as a substitute.)

Step 4

Parboil the Rice, then place in a sieve to drain out excess water.

Step 5

When preparing the vegetables: Wash all the vegetables. Dice the onion & set aside; Peel the carrots & cut into small cubes. Remove the seeds of the green bell peppers & cut into small cubes. Place the carrots & green peas in boiling water for 5 minutes, strain out and place in a bowl of cold water, leave to cool in the water, then pour into a sieve and set aside. (This method is called blanching)

Step 6

Place the reserved chicken stock into a large pot and bring to a boil. The stock should be at almost the same level as the rice, so that it dries up completely when the rice is done. You can add some water if the stock won't be enough to cook the Rice.

Step 7

As the stock begins to boil, add the parboiled rice, seasoning cubes, curry powder, garlic powder, onions and salt to taste. Leave to cook on medium heat until it's done. You can pour out the cooked rice into a wider pot and set aside.

Step 8

Heat up the Pure Vegetable Oil; add the carrots, peas, green pepper and diced liver/meat; then add a little curry & seasoning cube to taste. Stir fry for 1 min and pour into a bowl.

Step 9

The Rice is going to be fried in small batches, so you'll have to divide the stir-fried vegetables into equal portions. The size of your frying pan will determine how many portions you will have. Pour a portion of the stir-fried mix into the frying pan; add the cooked rice and stir-fry for about 2 minutes.

(Tip: Do not overcrowd the pan, make sure there is a little space in the pan so that you can move the rice around the pan for even distribution of heat.) Repeat this process for the remaining rice and vegetables mix.

Brown Rice & Pumpkin Salad

Ingredient

- 1 Cup Brown Rice Butternut Pumpkin, Skin Left On,
- Diced 3cm Cubes 70g Toasted Pine Nuts Or Slivered Almonds
- 3 Cups Baby Spinach Leaves
- 1/2 Red Onion, Peeled, Diced 5mm

- 2 Tbsp Lemon Juice Or White Balsamic Or To Taste
- 1 Tbsp Olive Oil,
- Salt & Pepper, To Taste

Method

1. Preheat oven to 180C and cook rice. To cook the rice, in a saucepan, add 1 cup of rice to 2.5 cups of cold water and bring to the boil. Reduce heat and simmer, covered for 25 minutes. Remove from heat and stand, covered for 5 minutes.

2. Lay pumpkin on a baking tray lined with baking paper. drizzle with olive oil and sprinkle salt and pepper over the top. Roast for about 40 minutes or until tender. Cool

3. Combine all the ingredients in a salad bowl and toss with clean hands. Serve immediately.

Vegan Dirty Rice

Equipment

- Large saucepan with lid
- Smaller saucepan with lid for cooking rice

Ingredients

- 1.5 cups basmati rice (raw)
- 3 cups vegetable stock
- 1 tsp extra virgin olive oil
- 1 large onion (finely diced)
- 3 stalks celery (finely diced)
- 3 green bell peppers (finely diced)
- 3 cloves garlic (smashed and minced)
- 2 tbsp sage (finely chopped)
- 14 oz vegan sausage (I used Beyond Meat, but any vegan sausage works here. Break it up into small bits by hand)
- 1/2 tsp smoked paprika
- 1 tbsp liquid aminos
- 1 tbsp Cajun seasoning
- Salt to taste

- 2 tbsp parsley (chopped)

Instructions

• Bring 2.5 cups of the vegetable stock to a boil in a saucepan, add salt and ground black pepper to taste, and add the raw rice. Once the stock comes back to a boil, add the rice, cover, and cook for 8 minutes.

• While the rice is cooking, in a large pot, heat the oil. Add the onions, celery, bell peppers, garlic and sage, add a dash of salt and ground black pepper, and saute for about five minutes until the vegetables are soft but not colored. Add the sausage and saute for a couple of minutes.

• Add the smoked paprika and liquid aminos and stir well, then fold in the cooked rice, the remaining half cup of vegetable stock, and the Cajun seasoning. Season with more salt and pepper if needed.

• Stir in the parsley and serve hot.

Note:

• To make this recipe with brown rice, use four cups of vegetable stock for the same quantity of rice, and let it cook 45 minutes over a low flame in a covered pot.

Instant Pot Mexican Rice

Ingredients

- 2 tablespoons olive oil
- 1 cup basmati rice, 200 grams, rinsed until water turns clear and drained until dry
- 1/2 red bell pepper, finely chopped
- 1 jalapeño, seeded & chopped
- 1 small red onion, finely chopped
- 2 garlic cloves, chopped
- 1/2 teaspoon cumin
- 1/2 teaspoon salt, or to taste
- 1 cup water, 8 oz
- 1 cup crushed canned tomatoes
- 2 tablespoons cilantro, minced
- Lime juice, optional

Instructions

- Rinse the rice until water turns clear. Then drain the water and let the rice dry.
- Press the saute button on your Instant Pot. Once it displays hot, add oil to the pot. Then add the rice and cook for 4 to 5 minutes until toasty.
- Add the bell pepper, jalapeno, onion, garlic and saute for 1 minute.
- Add the cumin, salt and saute for 30 seconds.
- Now add the water and stir to deglaze the pot (there shouldn't be anything sticking to the bottom).
- Add the canned crushed tomatoes on top. Do NOT STIR.
- Close the pot with its lid. Press the manual or pressure cook button and cook on high pressure for 5 minutes. The pressure valve should be in the sealing position.
- Let the pressure release naturally for 2 minutes and then do a quick pressure release.

- Open the pot, now carefully stir the tomato with the rice using a spoon. Cover pot with a glass lid, let it remain like that for 2 minutes.
- Remove the lid and add the cilantro. Fluff the rice with a fork. You may squeeze in some fresh lime juice.
- Serve Mexican Rice as a side or with beans or inside tacos, burritos!

Notes

*Tomato bouillon cubes or granules can be found in the Mexican food at your local grocery store. You could substitute chicken broth, but the rice won't have the same rich color.

Jamaican Rice and Peas

Ingredients

- 1 cup dried kidney beans rinsed, soaked overnight and drained
- 3 cups water
- 1 small onion, finely chopped
- 2 scallions, finely chopped
- 3 garlic cloves, minced
- 5 allspice berries
- 5 thyme sprigs
- 1 Scotch bonnet pepper
- 1/2 teaspoon grated fresh ginger
- Kosher salt
- Black pepper
- One 13.5-ounce can unsweetened coconut milk
- 2 cups long-grain white rice

Instruction

Step 1

In a large saucepan, cover the beans with the water and bring to a boil over moderately high heat. Stir in the onion, scallions, garlic, allspice, thyme, Scotch bonnet, ginger, 2 teaspoons salt and 1/2 teaspoon pepper. Stir in the coconut milk and bring to a simmer. Cover and simmer over low heat until beans are tender, about 1 hour; adjust the heat as necessary to maintain a gentle simmer.

Step 2

Stir in the rice, cover and simmer over low heat until the rice is tender and the liquid is absorbed, about 30 minutes. Remove from the heat and let steam for 10 minutes, then discard the thyme stems, allspice berries and Scotch bonnet. Using a fork, fluff the rice and beans and season with salt. Serve hot.

Turmeric Coconut Rice

Ingredients

- 2 cups brown rice, (Jasmine or Basmati) washed and drained
- 1 tablespoon coconut oil
- 1 small onion, finely chopped
- 2 cloves garlic, minced
- 1 teaspoon ground turmeric
- 2 green onions, chopped
- 2 sprigs of thyme
- 1 carrot, diced
- 1-15 oz can coconut milk
- 2 cups vegetable broth, or 1 vegetable bouillon plus 2 cups water
- 1/4 teaspoon Cayenne pepper, (optional)
- sea salt, to taste, (I used 1 1/2 teaspoons)
- 1/4 cup chopped cilantro, and lime juice, for garnish

Instructions

- Heat oil in a large pot on medium high, cook onion and garlic until soft about 3 minutes.

- Stir in turmeric, green onions, thyme, carrots and cook for a minute stirring constantly.
- Add rice and stir until rice is fully coated yellow. Add coconut milk, vegetable broth, cayenne pepper, and salt. (Make sure you add enough salt until it is flavorful).
- Bring to boil, cover and reduce to simmer on low for 50 minutes or until rice is tender. Remove from heat and keep covered for about 10 minutes.
- Fluff with a fork, stir in cilantro leaves and a squeeze of lime juice.

Notes

- I prefer to use Basmati, Jasmine or any long grain brown rice for a flakier rice. Short grain rice will most likely be too sticky.
- I usually cover the pot with a sheet of parchment paper underneath the pot cover to seal the pot and allow the rice to cook faster and flakier instead of being soggy.

Pineapple Fried Rice

Ingredients

- 1 cup (180 g) uncooked jasmine rice
- 2 cups (480 ml) water
- 1 pineapple
- 1 tablespoon (15 ml) fish sauce
- 1 tablespoon (15 ml) soy sauce
- 2 teaspoons (6 g) palm sugar
- 1 teaspoon (1 g) curry powder
- 2 tablespoons (45 ml) vegetable oil
- ¼ cup (30 g) minced red onion
- 2 tablespoons (20 g) minced garlic
- 2 teaspoons (4 g) minced ginger
- 4 ounces (120 g) shrimp, 31/40 count, peeled and deveined
- ½ cup (66 g) diced red bell pepper, ¼-inch dice
- ½ cup (65 g) green peas, fresh or frozen, defrosted
- ¼ cup (12 g) sliced green onions
- Black pepper, as needed for seasoning
- Cilantro leaves, for garnish

Directions:

- In a 3-quart sized saucepan, add rice and water. Bring to a boil and then turn down heat to a simmer and cover with a lid.
- Simmer rice for 10 to 12 minutes, or until all of the water is absorbed and rice is tender.
- Remove rice from the heat and allow to sit covered for 5 to 10 minutes.
- Fluff rice with a fork and allow to cool while preparing the pineapple fried rice ingredients.
- Cut the pineapple in half lengthwise and carve out wedges from both sides of the core.
- Carefully cut out the core, to create a hollow bowl. Scrape the inside flesh with a spoon if needed after removing the core.

- Cut the removed pineapple flesh into ½-inch pieces, reserving about 1 cup (7 ounces, 200g).
- In a small bowl mix together fish sauce, soy sauce, sugar, and curry powder.
- Heat a wok or large saute pan over high heat.
- Add the vegetable oil, once hot add the onions, ginger, and garlic, stir-fry for 30 seconds.
- Add the shrimp and cook until it turns pink in color, about 2 minutes.
- Add the bell pepper and peas, cook 1 minute.
- Add the rice, constantly stir to combine and cook for 2 minutes.
- Add the fish sauce mixture and stir to combine.
- Add the diced pineapple and green onions, stir to combine.
- Season rice with black pepper as desired.

- Transfer rice into pineapple bowl and garnish with cilantro leaves.

Printed in Great Britain
by Amazon

68357329R10038